GOD
IS
PERSONAL

HOW REAL IS GOD TO YOU

E D E M   D .   B R O W N

WESTBOW
PRESS®
A DIVISION OF THOMAS NELSON
& ZONDERVAN

WestBow Press books may be ordered through booksellers or by contacting:

WestBow Press
A Division of Thomas Nelson & Zondervan
1663 Liberty Drive
Bloomington, IN 47403
www.westbowpress.com
844-714-3454

Scripture taken from the King James Version of the Bible.

Scripture taken from the New King James Version® Copyright © 1982 by Thomas Nelson. Used by permission. All rights reserved.

Scripture quotations marked (NLT) are taken from the Holy Bible, New Living Translation, copyright ©1996, 2004, 2015 by Tyndale House Foundation. Used by permission of Tyndale House Publishers, a Division of Tyndale House Ministries, Carol Stream, Illinois 60188. All rights reserved.

ISBN: 978-1-6642-6750-3 (sc)
ISBN: 978-1-6642-6749-7 (e)

Print information available on the last page.

WestBow Press rev. date: 06/06/2022

CONTENTS

INTRODUCTION

There's a world that's looking for a God but don't know who He is. They search for him through superheroes and ancient mythology. Many seek ways to connect to the cosmic and supernatural forces all in search for peace and meaning to life.

One thing that many can agree on albeit through differing beliefs and religions is the presence of an existence higher than man. Natural disasters such as the recent COVID 19 pandemic, tsunamis and earthquakes put the power of man in perspective and it becomes clear that greater forces exists in this world.

Today we live in a time where more than ever, people are looking for an answer to some of life's toughest questions. Life is constantly throwing new questions at us, but humanity doesn't seem to know where to look. Many people are moving in all directions in desperate search of the right answer. It has become an endless search with the need to go farther and farther for answers. We live in a day and age where we are even going beyond earth for answers. Numerous organizations are venturing into space trying to make space travel a reality all in the hope it will satisfy curious minds. Friends, the answer does not lie in the most distant part of space and no satisfaction will be met.

So, whether through dreams, visions, prophecy, horoscopes or even the metaphysical as known in science, we as humans are designed to seek answers to fill the longing for more within us. The problem is some search their whole lives not finding it. King

Solomon with all the wisdom God gave him, went on a pursuit to find all the answers to life's questions. He searched everywhere he could and engaged in whatever was pleasing to him but still couldn't find true meaning to life, finally terming everything as vanity. How and when will man come to the place of satisfaction and contentment?

The Good news is that in this puzzle there is a living God. One who is the first, the premier! For there must always be a first in everything, a start, a charge, to maintain order or else chaos ensues. He is the One and only God of the heavens and the earth who knows all the answers to all questions, whether big or small. The answers that humanity needs and not necessarily those we want for our own parochial interests.

The problem ultimately becomes who this God is to us and how we know Him. We know various people have different views of God. Believing there is God is not enough but it's how you know Him.

This book came out of a desire to know this Great God personally. Not some fantasy or comic. Not heresy or someone else's God but to get to know this God for myself and relate to Him as such. 'God is Personal' will make God more real than ever to you and not just something or someone that is talked about. God is real and it's time for Him to be known as He wishes. May this book unlock you into a world of eternity and not what is fleeting.

1

GOD WANTS TO
GET PERSONAL

wholeheartedly believe that God the creator of the universe is Personal, which is the title of this book. Such a simple statement yet planted with such significance. The word personal speaks to unique, individual, separate, belongs to you, just to name a few. God desires a personal relationship with every one of His children. God is a God of fellowship, of the heart, of expression. He longs to get closer and closer until there is no level of separation between the two making one. So why personal? God wants to know you and wants you to know Him. That is what love is. He doesn't want to be afar off but involved deeply in the lives of His people. There's this image of God standing far off in heaven in the skies above and humanity on earth with a great divide between. He is high up and we are low down. Nothing could be farther from the truth. God is very interested in what goes on on earth, but even more very concerned about His Children's well-being. So again, why personal? Because that's what God wants. God wants to Get Personal.

God is Personal can seem controversial especially from a religious standpoint. It carries an audacity with it, the thought of the God of the universe being lowered to a single individual seems daring and demeaning, even disrespectful. Why bring God down to a single person's level and perspective? The immediate answer is the person of Jesus. You see, not only did God seek such a relationship with us but He sent His Son to die on the cross to make sure it happens. He sent Jesus to break every barrier and reveal His Heart to us. (John 3:14 - 16)

IT BEGAN AS RELATIONSHIP

It began in the Garden, where God had intimate fellowship with humanity. Adam and Eve were both naked, nothing hidden before God, having fellowship in the presence of God their Father who had created them. This was as personal as it got and there was no shame in their nakedness. This was perfect unison. Man and woman under their own will totally devoted to their Father. (A threefold cord cannot be easily broken).

However Satan working through the serpent sought to break that hedge by attacking their personal relationship with God or for more clarity, the person of their relationship. Satan's words interrupted the knowledge they had of their relationship with God creating some form of disconnection. The serpent first isolated the woman catching her alone and one is attacked easier when alone. The serpent attacked what she knew about her relationship with God, then the woman also influenced the man in acting against the relationship He had with the Father. All the enemy had to do to be successful was deceive Adam and Eve into questioning the knowledge they had of God.

> *Genesis 3:3 But of the fruit of the tree which is in the midst of the garden, God hath said, Ye shall not eat of it, neither shall ye touch it, lest ye die.*
> *Genesis 3:4 And the serpent said unto the woman, Ye shall not surely die*
> *(KJV)*

2

God had told them they will die while Satan said otherwise, creating doubt within the woman. The enemy deceived them by sowing words contrary to those of the Father, creating a conflict within them. This troubled the relationship and knowledge they had of the Father, putting Him in a different light where they began to question and doubt His Words. The enemy is very good at this, getting us to always question the Word of God.

This resulted in man disobeying God and a break in the natural relationship man had with God, hence widening the gap between them as they were sacked from the garden. The close intimacy and fellowship man had with God got broken in the garden of Eden. The close relationship man was born into and used to was now removed and replaced with an unknown distance and separation. This would have severe consequences for man because we were not created to be isolated from God. The enemy had succeeded in removing man from his place and position and driving him out from the presence of his Father and Creator. Today it's easy for many to identify as atheists and doubt the very existence of God and have little understanding of this Great God because man has come so far from God.

This is why the devil hates any personal relationship with God because through it we are welcomed back into His presence and the original plan of God for humanity.

2

WHAT SATAN ATTACKS

The same kind of scenario in the Garden played out again with the same intention by Satan, however this time it failed. Satan is a trickster who uses old and trusted methods of attack to catch his targets. These are devices and weapons of old. He attempted to attack Jesus just as He had attacked Adam and Eve. This was when Jesus was led out into the wilderness to be tempted by the devil before His earthly ministry began.

In all 3 temptations Satan sought to question Jesus's sonship which was His identity. Jesus derived His authority and power from His position as Son of God. The enemy knew if he could again corrupt this knowledge and understanding Jesus had, he would succeed in breaking their relationship and remove Jesus from His earthly assignment. However, Jesus was more than sure in His identity and held to it preciously, He was firmly acquainted with the Word from the father and used it to defeat Satan at His tricks.

Satan thrives in confusion, getting one to question the truth. He sows doubt in the mind, corrupting knowledge until it affects the heart which is where relationship is. He uses whatever means and by whoever to distort what you know about God (your conviction) until you start to wonder then wander. Remember how the enemy used even Peter, a disciple of Christ to prevent Jesus from going to the cross which was his assignment on earth (Matthew 16:23).

This is ultimately what the enemy is always after, to get you wondering until you become lost. It is very easy for a wonderer to become a wanderer. Take the story of Job, it was obvious to all that Job was a devout man who sought His God. This however never stops the enemy. A true enemy hates you even more when you do good. Satan desired to attack Job because of His heart for God. The devil hates those with a unique genuine relationship towards God. God bragged about Job's devotion to Him, and this infuriated the devil who only asked to do one thing; and that was to discredit God in the life of Job and see what happens. Everything Satan did to Job was to get Him to lose faith and disbelieve. The devil posited that Job knew and related to God only on account of the vast blessings He had received. Even the devil knows unshakable worship of God is not in the blessings He gives us. He understood what true devotion to God entailed and knew it had to be based only on the right knowledge of God which creates a strong bond and unbending conviction. The devil destroyed everything Job had, every blessing in his life and in the ensuing chapters Job continued to wonder what had gone wrong. He asked questions and grieved but I believe his heart never wandered from God because his devotion for God had matured beyond material things. He once said God gives and God takes (Job 1:21). Even when his wife and friends discouraged him, he chose to still believe in God. (Though He slay me yet will I trust Him, Job 3:15). He related to God not on the blessings but on whom God was.

One great thing that came from all his suffering was his revelation of God deepened. His revelation and knowledge of God expanded giving him a better understanding of God. How we ought to be desperate to know more of Him because our conviction will increase and relationship with Him strengthen. We will not waver but stand firm in the knowledge of who HE IS no matter the kind of storms that come our way. The heart of the child of God does not faint and even when life's storms come our way, we are able to come through refined and even better off with a testimony to our credit of the goodness and faithfulness of God. God never leaves us!

This is what the devil fears and why he attacks us persistently to create a distance between God and us. He creates circumstances to distort our revelation of God causing us to see Him in the wrong way. This ultimately will create a wrong relationship. We must not allow this and instead defend ourselves since we are not ignorant of the enemy's devices.

3

REVELATION LEADS TO RELATIONSHIP

In marriage there is something secret and unique the husband and wife must know about each other unknown to anyone else. There must be a special heartfelt reason you fall for that person. The popular saying goes beauty lies in the eyes of the beholder. Someone cannot describe the beauty for you, you must know it for yourself, always. When you stop knowing it yourself you become reliant on whoever you must hear it from. Always remember you cannot get your truth from people's opinions. Truth must always be received by you, not someone. You cannot believe what someone else determines as truth until you accept it as yours.

Jesus once asked his disciples who people said He was, to which the disciples responded with the various opinions of the people, which were wrong. He then asked who YOU say I am, to which Peter got the answer right that He was the Son of God. Peter had received the truth about Jesus through proper revelation. His truth was not related to what people believed about Jesus.

Revelation is that special secret that is received, it is like a secret code that bonds the sender to the receiver. Revelation ultimately must come from within not without. If someone must tell you, it will not stay because it is not yet yours. You will also not have the privilege of hearing it straight from the source where it doesn't leave. It must always become yours then it cannot be stolen. This is how conviction works. When the message must be passed from one man to the other, the message will eventually be distorted changing its meaning. But when everyone hears the message for themselves there's no reduction in value.

Just like marriage, each revelation of God is separate and unique. It must be your experience, not you experiencing someone else's. However, all revelation must be based on the truth of God's Word and that's where it becomes a shared experience.

If we take our marriage example, we can understand this better. Though every different marriage or couple can have their own unique story, there must still be a constitutional basis for it to be determined as legal. So, the beauty of personal stories and testimonies is for uniqueness, however the confines of God's word ensures a standard of truth and a basis of agreement among the church and in the Christian faith. As much as each individual relationship with God helps us to know different sides of Him, it must not become a different God.

It then becomes necessary how we receive revelation to ensure we don't start on a faulty foundation. Simply we don't want our relationship with God to be based on a lie but rather on truth.

HOW TO RECEIVE REVELATION

There is no revelation without God's Word. There's no God's Word without the Holy Spirit. However, this must be carefully understood. The first thing that happens before you give your life to Christ is to hear His Word. (Rom 10:19). Now there are many ways to hear the Word of the Lord; through music, books, sermons to name a few. When the Word of God meets a ready heart, the Word of God deposits in there giving room for the Spirit of God to stay and operate (parable of the sower). The Spirit of God cannot dwell in isolation, He needs to feed on the Word of God. This then brings life out of the Word or brings the Word to life. It is this life in the Word that births revelation in a special way. The one who is filled with the unadulterated Word of God is the one bound to be full of Godly revelation because the Spirit of God will be constantly at work in your life. The spirit in you will be very active with the words of God always coming to life in you, giving you new meaning always. The Spirit behind those words (Heb 4:12) connect to your spirit creating a bond or relationship unique and personal, relevant to the individual. The reason it must be personal is because revelation is connected to purpose. God will relate to you specially based on your purpose. Following this process is a sound way of ensuring you stay within the confines of scripture in establishing a relationship with God and ensures true revelation through the Word of God.

So, then there's still the question of:

What happens to fellowship among believers if it's all about personal worship?

Finding God for yourself and relating to Him personally can still be problematic, because if we all relate to God personally (even while staying within the confines of scripture) then what becomes of fellowship?

The problem is not in corporate worship or coming together in fellowship but it is the tendency for God to be lost in the midst of the congregation and instead replaced by man's creation where that personal connection with God gets lost.

Personal worship and corporate worship should fundamentally be no different as both are directed at the same God. Worshipping God on my own should be no different in doing so with others, as both must be in spirit and truth.

Unfortunately, the usual case sees personal worship and devotion to God get lost in the corporate gathering. This is wrong as joining with believers should be an extension of personal worship. When the two begin to either conflict or replace the other then there are dire consequences for the body of Christ.

I have seen many people identify as Christians and filling the pews of the church get to bed at night feeling ever so distant from God with some not even knowing how to relate or engage Him. While others always have to rely on their pastors before going to God in prayer even for the simplest things. Often with such people, the heart can feel so far while doing things connected to their spiritual lives like praying, fasting or outreach. It can easily become routine and sometimes even feeling like a task or chore. Often it gets to a time that for some, God doesn't seem or feel real enough to them anymore. There are several reasons I focus on the personal nature of God in this book so people can gain the right knowledge to connect with the Good Lord in their very hearts.

With all this said about our individual worship, God is still God of the Church and as noted above there is still the need for right fellowship. In the ensuing chapters we will see how to merge our personal walk with the greater group of believers as we cannot be alone.

4

THE PRETENCE OF THE CROWD

There is something I have observed very strongly that I call the pretence of the crowd. It is very difficult to truly analyse what a crowd is made up of. The character of a crowd can be very deceptive. One of the easiest things to sway is a crowd, it is not difficult at all. All you need to do is to create a controlling factor that will keep the crowd acting a particular way. This is what goes on in most of the church now. There are various sizes of congregation all with various constitutions. This is usually separated according to denominations, but even same denominations can be run differently. But no matter the number of denominations and churches, the problem with most of these is still the same because of the pretence of the crowd.

THE PROBLEM WITH A CROWD

There are various problems with a crowd we must be careful of. One of the things I have become aware of is the difference between a crowd and an association. To be an associate is to be an invested partner while a crowd member just makes a number. And because of how easily swayed crowds can be the individual involved has no say. Questions are not asked, feedback is not encouraged, people just move and sway as controlled.

THE NUMBERS GAME

Today we yearn to be fruitful and multiply and increase our numbers but instead of through growth, it has become because of the deception of the crowd. We play the numbers game where the larger the crowd the more attractive it looks because it appears more impactful. So, there's a large penchant and desire for numbers from both sides of the coin. There's an emphasis on numerical growth primarily over individual growth. All the structures are designed to push this agenda consequently leading to little attention to the individual wellbeing, which is the state of each heart and soul.

The pulse of the church cannot be measured by a crowd response. The heart of each person must be attended to individually. This can only be done by emphasising on personal relationship with God. However, the greatest issue with this is the fear of the removal of the controlling factor. The resistance to this is largely based on a similar situation the Pharisees went through.

There was an iron fist on the worship of God during the time of Jesus on earth. The Pharisees and their chief priest and other religious groups controlled every bit of worship. They sacked people from temple worship just for challenging their stance like the blind man Jesus healed (Matthew 15:14).

Jesus on the other hand always looked to break their hold on Godly worship by pointing to true worship of God being more than synagogues and temples but in spirit and truth, of the heart. He referred to the religious leaders as blind guides who don't enter themselves and don't want anyone else to enter (John 9:22). What a damning testimony of the leadership of the day. Needless to say the Pharisees hated Jesus and had him killed for the Truth.

Today the same thing happens, that same antichrist spirit is still in operation, even stronger. Just like Christianity had to be wrestled from the hands of the Catholic church hundreds of years ago by great men and women of God who were seeking the truth for themselves such as Martin Luther, today there are other hijackers of God's church by even more dangerous and subtle means. These hijackers come in the form of titles and anointing which give some form of rank. With this seemingly unmovable hierarchy, all forms of unscrupulous people using the guise of position and titles unfortunately become the gap between the people and God meanwhile that gap is only reserved for one person, Jesus Christ.

Just as at one point in history the Bible could only be read and owned by few, so now it seems only a few have special and full access to God. This is a wrong, evil, and misplaced notion that has been accepted by many to the detriment of the church. This prevents most people from seeking and knowing God deeply for themselves. This is what God would have most, special unbridled access to all His children. This is what the Church must look like. Not one going for many but each going for themselves to see the King. A special relationship with each child. What a sight to behold that will be.

5

WHAT IS THE RIGHT CONTROL?

The question then becomes how to maintain a right standard in what a personal relationship with God looks like. Surely, we cannot allow just anything to pass as a relationship if we are to have unity. Having no control over the church could see liberty turn into licentiousness and that too is a disaster. However, having a wrong control factor also leads to human establishment replacing the worship of God. What then becomes the best way of ensuring everyone has a correct relationship with God with one standard.

We can learn a lot from studying church history. Before the great Protestant reformation that transformed the church in the 1500s, it was largely known that the Catholic Church was riddled with many troubles. There was great stigma and negativity surrounding the church however it must be noted that it was not the entire church that had a problem. There were many God fearing people in those days but there was a largely corrupted hierarchy seeking to manipulate matters from both in front and behind. Many voices spoke against these bad characters who were headquartered in Rome and the damage it was doing to the church at large but it fell on deaf ears to those who seemed untouchable then.

The problem wasn't that the whole Catholic Church was corrupt, it was that those who controlled it were. It is the controllers who had to change.

The issue has always been the controlling factor. More important than the crowd are the controllers of the crowd. Jesus Himself said strike the shepherd and the sheep will scatter. So, the great question quickly becomes what is the right control and what is the best way of controlling the people and the church of God?

THE HOLY SPIRIT: THE CONTROL

One of the biggest problems I have come to see is the church not treating the Holy Spirit as an actual person. Our failure to see and recognize the Holy Spirit as He truly is, that is as a person and the Head of the Church here on earth. The Church needs to wake up to this truth, so the hierarchy becomes clear to every believer. You cannot have the Holy Spirit and not recognise this truth. Having the Holy Spirit of God makes you to realise Him as the First and Premier Person of the Church above all else.

Take the day of Pentecost, the instruction was clear to wait for the Holy Spirit to come before the church can be birthed. Now what was the first thing to happen, the entrance and move of the Holy Spirit with evidence. There was a clear outward appearance, as the sound of a mighty rushing wind. Spiritually there was the tongues of fire on each believer.

So first and foremost came the work of the Holy Spirit in the person, this was then followed by the speaking of other tongues, an outward sign to identify the working of the Spirit in each believer. Then came Peter amid all this by the same inspiration of the Holy Spirit to speak thereby bringing more souls to the kingdom, the increase.

There was a clear order. The Spirit of God first, His Working in the life of the believer then the choosing of the servants for different works.

This is the way the controlling factor is meant to work in the kingdom of God. Not by rules, constitution, doctrines, or any other means. Today you have so many denominations and churches all with varying ways of doing things, mostly conflicting one another.

The division in today's church is deafening and clear for all to see. This is because of the wrong controlling forces put in place.

I am not so naïve not to understand the place of men and leaders in the plan of God, but I am convinced that many of these people end up knowingly or unknowingly taking the place of the Holy Spirit. Even though God uses men and women mightily, it is my belief just like Jesus exemplified with the Great Commission, the grace is supposed to have a multiplying effect spreading to all and feeding all just like the three loaves and two fishes and not just stay on one person. Notwithstanding, there will surely be positions but a sure sign of the Spirit at work is the higher the position the larger the service and the more people are lifted. Not the other way where the more the individual is served, and the more people lift him up. Jesus said it's the gentiles who lord over their people.

6

THE STRONGHOLD
OF TRADITION

The worst thing about corporate worship is when tradition kicks in. The stronghold of tradition is when anything new is frowned upon. Anything new is fresh, original, and unique. It may take some time getting used to and always calls for attention just like it happened on the day of Pentecost. It is key to experience renewal periodically just like an eagle does to maintain its strength. (Is 40:31)

One great evil of tradition is the removal of liberty. Tradition is a prison. Scripture tells us where the Spirit of the Lord is there's liberty (2 Cor 3:17), but liberty for what exactly? To worship in spirit and in truth (John 4:24).

Due to the personal nature of the Holy Spirit indwelling God's children, the worship of God is still personal even when in a group.

Let's take the example of a couple's retreat which sees various marriage folk gather at a set location to rejuvenate their union. It will be a major mistake to want each couple to have the same exact experience because you don't know the different situations. The couples will also be wrong looking at other couples and trying to copy and imitate their experience. For each couple to fully utilise the program it must be a unique experience which is focused on their inward problems. This then leads to a shared outcome of growth and renewal.

This is the situation in most of our churches. We have a one cap fits all attitude. That is tradition. It is fear of releasing the people, it has become a jail. Of course, there's the other extreme where liberty turns to licentiousness but that will be dealt with further on.

A hospital cannot run effectively with one medication for all. There is consultation, tests, diagnosis and then medication for different treatments but the same result is desired which is good health and healing.

Stubborn leaders, stubborn churches and a stubborn people maintain traditional methods even when the desired results are no longer achieved. These are done through procedures that are said to have once worked ignorant of the changing times. Just imagine the digital age we live in with a church that refuses to introduce technology into their services. They will certainly find some scripture to wrongfully back their decision. Great organisations have done this and failed, falling into oblivion.

The temptation is always to stick to what once was, and what once worked but there's a beauty in renewal. Renewal does not change the content, only the appearance. An eagle does not keep the old but once dependable parts but sheds them for new ones so it can maintain its high altitude. We don't keep the old and weakened but are to be continually renewed with fresh vitality to soar higher and higher.

A similar example I can think of is our old church hymns. Powerful to the core but so are the fresh new songs we have today. Most are adaptations of the hymns but to a new modern sound creating a fresh ambience. God loves things fresh, new and effective. He said behold I do a new thing (Isaiah 43:19) and eye hath not seen nor ear heard (1 Cor 2:9); God is very interested in life and life in abundance so any sign of death is abhorrent to Him and this is why He is a God of revival. (2 Cor 5:17)

7

CORPORATE WORSHIP

Worship is the expression of our faith. It is the means by which we display our heartfelt love to our God. Corporate worship is a shared experience. This is often forgotten because of selfish intents and motives. Anything that is shared well must be selfless. Take the example of sharing a birthday cake or sweets to a group of young people. Everyone is happy when it is shared equally but anything else would surely lead to dissatisfaction. Jesus always preached about selflessness in the Kingdom of God. The ability to put others ahead of yourself. His very life on earth defined that vividly. (Love your neighbour as yourself and the washing of the feet are two examples).

In corporate worship the only thing that guarantees success is when everyone is lost in the unity of the group. It must move progressively from 'my' personal to 'our' personal, my experience to our experience. Each person is still experiencing God intimately on their own but the power of numbers which speaks to agreement intensifies and magnifies the experience. The bible speaks of the power of agreement in if two agree on a thing it is established in heaven and a threefold cord cannot be easily broken. Multiplication always leads to a multiplied effect. Your worship of God carries mighty power but when our worship is all tied together in one accord, it is virtually impossible to stop. You get lost in such an atmosphere and everything becomes shared. My Father finally becomes Our Father and burdens become lighter because of the shared weight. Individuals dissipate to make room for the congregation. Selfishness disappears to the mighty spirit of selflessness which is Christ. It is all so spiritual, and the results go beyond measure sometimes leaving a lasting impact for years.

It must not be forgotten that the reason for fellowship is the shared love of God. The people who are to benefit most from corporate worship are the lesser. Jesus reminded his disciples that in His kingdom the leaders who are the higher are to serve the congregation. He told Peter three times to feed His sheep representing the early church as a sign of His love towards Jesus.

Believers gathering shouldn't be for a few people and definitely shouldn't be for the elite and high in society. When Jesus began His earthly ministry, He announced what His assignment entailed, and it was clear who was the target of His ministry.

(The Spirit of the Lord GOD is upon me; because the LORD hath anointed me to preach good tidings unto the meek; he hath sent me to bind up the broken-hearted, to proclaim liberty to the captives, and the opening of the prison to them that are bound; Isaiah 61:1)

A very big error in today's church is the emphasis and attention placed on the rich. This is against the order of God but very fitting with that of man. God places greater focus on the low in society so they can be lifted and the gap of inequality closed. Concentrating on one group and leaving the other is like forgetting a part of the body while bathing, eventually the neglect will show on the whole body or at least discomfort the other parts of the body. For corporate worship to work it must be all inclusive and equally shared with the higher serving the lower by the example of Christ.

BECOMING YOUR OWN CHURCH

Becoming your own church means the church must start with you. Every Christian must have a personal altar they service by constant sacrifice and worship to God. This altar is their heart and must be kept clean and pure for meaningful devotion. Romans 12:1-3 says we must become the sacrifice. For something to become personal, it must take up space in your heart and just as the heart helps pump blood throughout the whole body, so the heart must spread the love of God around everything you do. The Bible directs to guard your heart for out of it comes all the ways of life (Proverbs 4:23). The heart is the altar of every believer to which true worship must start. This keeps our worship of God and all we do honest to Him. It prevents us from doing things selfishly which is the innate nature of man. A believer must do everything for the benefit of the Kingdom of God, we must serve Him from our hearts willingly and not begrudgingly. Not giving in to the temptation to serve our individual desires or other men.

People wishing to serve God who become indifferent or nonchalant do so because they begin to focus their worship elsewhere and not the Lord. There are many who worship with their minds, their intellect, they reason it out. But that can't last since that is carnality and not spirituality and the carnal mind person cannot please God since their desire is on earthly things. Christianity is a long journey that involves many different roads, many which you are unaware of because your vehicle is not being driven by you but the One you've given your life to. He knows the destination and that is why your heart must be always to Him. Many things will aim to take your heart away making one indifferent or focus elsewhere. We are told of how Solomon who began well in his service to God got distracted along the way because his many wives took his heart away from God. We must be careful of idol worship where we serve multiple gods other than the one true God, Jesus. This is where God ceases to be personal. The light and fire of your altar grows dim until it quenches. God wants you passionate, therefore He seeks your heart, your sacrifice, your reasonable act of worship.

8

SACRIFICE

Any church, community or organisation that lacks sacrifice is devoid of proper relationship. Traditions, rituals, and even religious activities cannot breed sacrifice. The bible says where your treasure is, there your heart will be also (Matthew 6:21) meaning whatever you treasure or cherish becomes dear to your heart. What you don't cherish or treasure cannot be taken to heart. It becomes eye service and does not emanate from the heart.

> *You hypocrites! Isaiah was right when he prophesied about you, for he wrote, 'These people honor me with their lips, but their hearts are far from me.(Matthew 15:7-8)*

The Christian journey is one centered around sacrifice. It will crop up in everything we are to do and the faster we develop our hearts to be broken to this truth the better our walk will go. Our example of Christ gives us the grace and meaning we need to live a life of service and selflessness by the help of the Holy Spirit. It is impossible to this of our own, like Peter who though willed to serve his Christ was a slave to self however after the day of Pentecost rose to the height of service. We cannot highlight and emphasize enough that the Christian lifestyle is one of service, willingness to the cause of our King. This must be ingrained in the fibre of our spirits.

This is an important point to speak about the way we evangelise and reach out as Christians. It is important to first note that there isn't one method of winning souls to the Kingdom of God. Peter was called by Jesus after performing a miracle in His life while Paul was struck down by Jesus on the Damascus Road. Two important personalities in Christianity converted in different ways. However, note the similarities in both their conversions. In Matthew, Peter is called by Jesus with the understanding that he will be in service to God (Matthew 4:18-19). The same is said of Paul in Acts of the Apostles when he is told by Jesus he will live a life of service (Acts 9:5-6, 15). Both were drafted into the kingdom of God not based on wealth, healing, fame or otherwise but in the knowledge of a life of service. The Kingdom of God is service to our Master with the knowledge that all other things will be added. (Matthew 6:33)

Now a key scripture used in evangelism today is in Matthew 22, the story of the Big Banquet. It has largely played a role in the way the church wins souls today. Christians are generally encouraged to bring new souls to church at all costs, to compel them to come. As well-meaning as this seems, it can end problematically if done without understanding.

A relationship with God cannot be forced and if we want to see genuine love, then people of God it must be based on relationship and not any kind of force. If anyone comes to God based on force, the same amount of force if not more is needed to keep them. One can and should be compelled to come to church but by Godly means and not human wisdom or tactics. Just like the two examples above, commitment to Jesus is not child's play and should not be undermined to just get people to fill the pews of the churches just to add to the numbers. It is of no advantage to the Kingdom of God if there are large numbers and crowds at our services but with no proper commitment and understanding of what the gospel demands.

I believe the scripture speaks to position and of using one's position to get people into the kingdom. Using one's wealth, resources, and efforts to save dying souls from hell and eternal damnation. To see a dying world and do something about it, to be the salt and light of this world, but the rest must be done by the individual. It must always remain an invitation and left for them to answer, not a force or intimidation that ignores their response. For example, a manager of a business has a unique position of seeing people's needs and extending a hand of fellowship to them by directing them to a banquet prepared by the Lord for them where they can eat and never hunger again. I believe the church has a great mandate of finding the need and impressing it on them the need to attend the great banquet, but we must be careful of forcing them into a relationship with God and accepting Christ as Saviour. Remember Jesus said Behold He stands at the door and knocks (Rev 3:20), the response must always be allowed for the individual to make. Each must make that decision to sacrifice their own life to Jesus.

9

THE IMPORTANCE
OF THE SOURCE

There's a source to everything, a beginning just as there's an end. Great lives, gigantic trees, they all begin as a seed. A mighty river has its source from seas or oceans and is additionally helped by rainwater. For any existence to continue, it must stay connected to its source and continue to be fed. No building can remain steady without staying rooted to its strong foundation.

This is same for our Christian walk and spiritual lives. The source of our spirit beings is God given and breathed. Just as our physical seed comes from our parents, our spiritual life on earth starts through being reborn in Christ. This is when we put an end to our old worldly way of life and awaken to new lives in Christ through the power and work of the Holy Spirit. Our spirit comes alive by which we can be led by the Holy Spirit. This connects us back to God who is our true source of life eternal. It's imperative to maintain a strong connection to continually prosper through various seasons of life.

This is because the strength of connection to the source influences the wellbeing of the connected body. It is not just about being connected but the strength of the connection. In technology, a WIFI connection will give you access to the internet but the strength of it gives you more speed on the internet. I would like to give two scenarios using a water reservoir to properly understand our connection to God our Source.

Imagine a water reservoir with a large storage situated at the top of a hill with a community of houses at the base of the hill. Now proximity to the reservoir will be a factor to strength of flow. The closer you are to the reservoir the stronger the flow into your house. If you are farther away from the hill, the water will have to pass through several others before reaching you hence your water reception will be relatively weaker. The water flow weakens the more houses it passes through before reaching yours.

This is like our relationship with God. This is the reason I stress on proximity to God our Source. The closer the connection the more personal it becomes leading to a stronger relationship. Too far and too distant the more the relationship will lose meaning. We must not allow too many things to come between us and the source no matter what those things are. This is why God sent so many warnings concerning idols.

In Exodus when Moses goes up Mount Horeb, Aaron who stays back with the people of Irael builds an image of a golden calf through which they will worship God. For Aaron he had not built a strong relationship enough to withstand the pressure of the people without Moses there. Both cases show the necessity of developing direct engagement with God especially for when the winds blow. God shows through Jesus the kind of direct relationship He wants with all of us with Jesus being the only mediator.

We must be careful of not allowing far too many obstacles between us and God. It will certainly diminish the strength in connection to God our Source. Practically we must resist anything becoming an idol in our lives. An idol is anything that becomes a medium or checkpoint between God and you. You must then seek permission from that thing before you worship God. It can be a job, spouse, law, habit; anything at all that prevents you from freely accessing God right. Jesus said in John 14:6, I am the Way, the Truth and Life and no one gets to the Father except through Me. He is then the only One we must get through before God. Nothing more, nothing less.

Everything and everyone else can only be a help and not the object of our worship. Even the Holy Spirit is a Helper to us in our worship of God. Of course, in order and priority, the Holy Ghost is the greatest and most important Helper we have without which we cannot worship the Lord. We must endeavour to remain strongly connected to God our Source.

Back to the water reservoir illustration, imagine due to an obstruction in the pipe flow, supply of water from the reservoir is shut. The water flow does not immediately cease in your house due to the amount of pressure already in the pipes from the reservoir and it will take some time before the water stops running. So, you see that even though the reservoir has stopped supplying water directly to you, you keep experiencing some flow of water unaware of the fact that the main supply has been shut. The water keeps flowing but the pressure (strength) begins to reduce until it eventually stops.

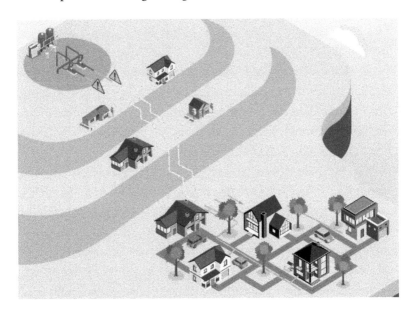

This is what happens in our spiritual lives. There is an important thing to notice here, the closer you are to the source is the quicker you realise supply has ceased but the farther you are the longer it takes. Having a strong personal relationship with God allows you to notice the differences in strength and quickly adjust. It is vital to know when your relationship with God is becoming strained and begin to work on it. We must pay attention to our spiritual lives not allowing it to decay to a very bad state before taking care of it. Staying well connected to the source means we are always servicing the connection to maintain its strength.

Unaware to us, destructions and even blockades can appear in our lives creating a gap between us and God and eventually cut us away. Unfortunately, this leads to our spiritual lives drying up. We sometimes experience underwhelming supply to our spiritual lives leaving us feeling short-changed and seeking for more. We can get the feeling that our God is just not enough because the source is out of supply but we have unknowingly been cut from the source, being forced to flow on bare minimum or in some cases nothing at all but only memories of the so called glory days.

Instead we should remove all obstacles and blockades whatever they may be in our lives blocking us from our Godly supply. Our Father in heaven has so much supply of peace, love, joy and every heavenly blessings to keep us victorious in this life. There are many things seeking to constantly distract us and keep us from reconnecting to our Source of life; we must pray to disconnect from everything that influences us negatively and enter the rest that comes from Our Source. Beautiful worship music, anointed preaching and books filled with the Word of God are all able to help us to reconnect.

There has been one common foe to believers over the generations on reaching the goal of a beautiful relationship with God just as was established in the Garden of Eden. There is one barrier all will have to cross if they are to reach an authentic more excellent way which is a relationship through Jesus to the Father. That barrier is TRADITION.

10

THE BREAKING OF TRADITION

Tradition is one huge weight, seemingly unsurmountable in most cases. It weighs down like an albatross on whoever it holds. Tradition in spirituality is even worse. Most people like to refer to this as religion because of the set of rules it represents but tradition is much larger. Tradition can affect even the most spiritual with the Holy Ghost. Take Peter who even after the day of Pentecost, being one of the chief apostles still held on to tradition on two separate occasions. One against the Lord Himself during a vision to break it and the other being when Paul himself criticised him for being hypocritical concerning the Gentiles and the Jews. We will touch on these two cases and then culminate it with the revelation given in John 4 by Jesus Christ.

During Moses's encounter at the burning bush, he asked God what His name was and the name he was given was I AM THAT I AM (Exodus 3:14). God revealed Himself to Moses, the children of Israel and all who were to know as I AM strongly connected to His name YHWH. The name is endless, infinite, and impossible to define or confine. It feels always present, ever new, a fitting description of God. Whereas everything else can be measured, this God cannot, He is timeless. This was the name by which God introduced Himself to the children of Israel forever.

Exodus 3:14-15 (KJV)
And God said unto Moses, I AM THAT I AM: and
he said, Thus shalt thou say unto the children of Israel,
I AM hath sent me unto you. And God said moreover
unto Moses, Thus shalt thou say unto the children of
Israel, The LORD God of your fathers, the God of
Abraham, the God of Isaac, and the God of Jacob,
hath sent me unto you: this is my name for ever, and
this is my memorial unto all generations.

The importance of this name and encounter is because as discussed earlier man likes what they can control, even to the point of God Himself. This is what religion does, binding God to a set of rules and regulations to which He must adhere to. We try to restrict God to a program or organisation that is planned to our way of life.

We then keep this under lock and key, never evolving or growing, getting rid of all forms of liberties ensuring nothing changes the status quo, not even welcoming questions nor conversations. It becomes a computer program that is just fed to everyone, no questions asked. From generation to generation nothing changes and everything is guarded. Sounds familiar, this is tradition and it is found everywhere. Tradition ultimately is a prison.

Christianity and tradition do not go together for this was one of the very things the Christ came to remove. Right from when Jesus was a boy asking questions in the temple to working miracles on the Sabbath when He began His earthly ministry, it would seem Jesus was very unconventional and at times breaking tradition. He was strongly opposed by the Pharisees and other religious leaders of the day. Why was Jesus always at war with them one would ask, the answer is in Mark 7:8:

> *Mark 7:8 (KJV)*
> *For laying aside the commandment of God, ye hold the*
> *tradition of men, as the washing of pots and cups: and*
> *many other such like things ye do.*

It was because of how they treated God's Word. The pretence and hypocrisy about their behaviour concerning the things of God caused Jesus to call them white washed tombs. Looking clean on the outside but dirty and dead on the inside. It is only the hold and grip of tradition that can do this. No matter how outdated or counterproductive their belief systems were to the relevance of the times, they were never willing to bend. They had become blindly fixed, stiff-necked, stagnant in growth and averse to any form of revelation. Tradition is the enemy to revelation.

In the book of Acts, Jesus appeared in a dream to Peter where all kinds of animals were given to him to kill and eat. Peter being a strong and committed Jew, it was against their laws and customs and he turned it down even when a voice from heaven commanded him to eat. Later it was revealed to him by the Spirit of God how the gentiles were to become a part of God's kingdom through him. If Peter was to have stuck to traditional values he will never have done the will of God. Oh how many of us find ourselves out of the will of God because of old, foregone, quite frankly useless traditions. Some corners of the world truly have some very horrendous traditions that are so backward such as FGM in some African societies.

Peter declared that from birth he had never eaten anything unclean to which God responded don't call unclean what the He God Almighty had made clean. Such a profound statement on how we as men can limit the omnipotent God by our ignorance. One can see how we've only touched the tip of how much damage tradition is doing to the body of Christ, the people of God and even humanity. What are we in our own small ways labelling us unclean that God may be wanting to do something about? What are we holding on to that God is trying to rebirth and renew? God is a God of reformation not tradition.

Just as God is always revealing Himself as I AM and not I WAS, how we ought to carefully examine ourselves that we do not become caught and trapped in the yeast of the Pharisees Jesus warned about.

11

DEALING WITH THE PRESSURES OF TRADITION

P aul strongly condemned Peter for bowing to tradition through pressure and like the Pharisees relegating God's Word to the background (Gal 2:11-13). The Spirit of God operates best through liberty which is willingness and not force and Paul clearly understood this. There is always great pressure and temptation to do what everyone else is doing joining the yoke of the crowd and refusing to step out into the freedom of God's Word. Jesus said my burden is light and my yoke is easy (Matthew 11:30). Everything else comes from the devil and is meant to keep us in bondage including tradition. It leads to bad news and Peter was guilty of this if not for the intervention of Paul. He was doing the right thing until he became affected by the presence of the Jews and joined the pretence of the crowd moving away from truth. How daring this spirit of tradition is contending even against chief apostles who walked in the presence of Jesus. This was the same Peter who caught the revelation of who the Christ was and was blessed for that. How careful we ought to be. In the church, in homes, workplaces, marriages, nations, tradition is everywhere and must be eradicated for the Spirit of God to freely move.

You can be 10, 50 or even 100 years and still be affected by tradition. It only grows as you age and the stronghold becomes harder to break. The root thickens, your heart holds even firmer to those beliefs never wanting to let go. The grip of tradition is deadly and that is why without being properly born again, you cannot effectively deal with this spirit well, there will always be remnants left.

The worse thing about this is it's so strong in the church now because disciples are not letting go and becoming new creation. Even the place of deliverance is so entangled on traditional grounds and methods. God help us.

JESUS FREES US FROM TRADITION'S HOLD..........

In John 4, personally one of my favourite scriptures, we can clearly see the personality of Jesus as far as traditions are concerned. Jesus the tradition breaker appears on the scene.

In the story the woman at the well was going about her usual business before her encounter with Jesus. He asked her for water to drink already breaking tradition because they were of contending tribes as she was a Samaritan and a woman at that. It must be emphasized Jesus had no time for human tradition. He never puts man's word above the Father. The only word that truly mattered was what God had to say.

The woman had married four times and was currently living in adultery, yet Jesus had asked her for water because His purpose is redemption. He said he came not to condemn but to save (John 3:17).

......INTO THE FREEDOM OF TRUE WORSHIP

The importance of this scripture is in the explanation of true worship. True worship is not in place or location after all Jesus instructed us to pray in our closet or secret place (Mat 6:6). It is not in the amount of time or even how much you give. They are all parts of worship but not what it should become about or how it should be determined. True worship certainly does not depend on how long something has been done for. John 4:24 details what true worship is:

God is spirit, and those who worship Him must worship in spirit and truth."

Jesus says in Mat 18:20 that where two or more are gathered in **His Name**, there He will also be.

The woman at the well told Jesus they worship at Samaria because their fathers worshipped there because of Abraham while the Jews insisted on worship in Jerusalem because of the temple. Jesus simply responded that she worships out of ignorance. How profound a warning to all who confess to be worshipping God.

She doing something because it had been so for so long did not make it right. She worshipped what she did not know because there was no personal connection. She was just doing it, it was tradition.

True worshippers do so in spirit and truth where there is a connection, and not tradition. Not worship because our ancestors or grandfathers worshipped there, otherwise that becomes idol worship. Instead worship out of revelation, that is the spirit and truth. Jesus spoke and His words gave this woman a revelation she had not seen before, breaking the hold of tradition. Tradition and revelation are enemies so encountering one dislodges the other.

She after realising who Jesus was, the source of all life, the rivers of living water, the cup that never dries, broke all ignorance in her, opened her eyes to the truth and she immediately chose life in Christ over tradition. So many times, tradition hinders our healing, breakthrough and deliverance. For some, tradition has even blocked salvation like those in other religions.

The woman dealing with the issue of blood after trying everything else had to move and try something new, something different. The devil loves for us to stay confined to our old and to never be released to the I AM who changes all things. No revival can take place anywhere when the rule of tradition is in place. Not in nations, governance, communities, schools, churches, workplaces, marriages and anywhere else. Anywhere tradition rules, revival which brings in the new, refreshing is blocked and the old, dead persists. This must not be so. We must be influencers as Jesus was. Always bringing new life where we are. May there be a fresh outpouring as on the Day of Pentecost inside you.

12

THE PROBLEM OF "OWNING GOD"

'Owning God' is the most dangerous thing a man can attempt to do and is the backbone to tradition. This is one way tradition entered the church. We would explore what this concept means and its adverse effects on the Body of Christ in general especially in deterring people from seeking a real relationship with God.

So, what is owning God? As discussed earlier, a controversial side of making God personal is the danger of reducing God to an individual understanding and that understanding growing to become a doctrine and constitution placed on a larger group of people. There is nothing compared to the strength and connection of relationship but a major risk always becomes the spirit of familiarity and losing the awe and splendour that must be attributed to everything God does. No matter how great and mighty an experience is, there is the tendency to become less fascinated by it after multiple times and over an extended period. I love nature so I can imagine the awe and splendour of the Victoria Falls or the power and magnificence of Mount Everest, however I do wonder what it means for the people who live in those areas, is there a feeling of familiarity? You see there's a risk of becoming so familiar to great things that human as we are, we begin to take them for granted forgetting how marvellous those very things once were to us.

Going further, encountering greatness is very humbling. There's a large sense of gratitude because there's a clear realisation of positions. Whether it is in meeting a dignitary, or the boss during a job interview or even being present at an event where history is made, it is seen as wonderful and awesome that you were there and can be unforgettable.

But what happens when the door is opened to you and you become part of that greatness. Suddenly you are part of that government, top organisation and institution. You are part of the power play and are rubbing shoulders with various levels of greatness. You have gained access to the secret places behind the scenes responsible for the wonders you once stood in awe of. You move from a place of no responsibility to being a part of the success. Do you still appreciate the greatness the same or everything in your perspective shifts because of your new position? I hope the picture is becoming clear on how familiarity can alter experience.

So it is with becoming so used to the things of God, it may never start as the intention but increasing levels of familiarity undoubtedly fuels this journey arriving at the wrong destination of taking ownership and control of God, that is thinking one can control God and know how to use Him for your own interests. To properly understand how this ownership of God can take place we will look at the example of the children of Israel. Tracing it from their encountering of God in the beginning all the way to their continuous idolatry and failure to properly worship God as is pleasing to Him.

It is difficult to accurately describe or put in words what an encounter with God is like. Apart from unique where its like you the only person in the room, an encounter with God is always impacting, like a collision leaving you deformed (not the same). It acts like a trademark of God on each person like Moses after encountering God's presence on Mt Sinai had his face radiant with the Glory of the Lord. Every Christian, every believer must continuously pray for an encounter with God because no matter how great an encounter, one is not enough.

THE POWER OF AN ENCOUNTER

After a person has an encounter, it has a profound effect on them. The initial encounter a person has with a thing leads to either a positive or negative relationship with it. This is because of the power of revelation. Revelation is how you see and perceive a thing. An encounter leads to revelation which then leads to relationship, either a good or bad one. The same principle occurs in Christianity and this is how we are to start our personal relationship with Jesus Christ. Each Christian must go through this process right to establish the right foundation. The problem and danger however occur where there is no encounter or the encounters cease. This is dangerous for many reasons.

The children of Israel in Egypt decided to put all their Egyptian gods away and follow the Great and Mighty God who appeared to them. All the power this great and mighty God had displayed was enough to earn their allegiance forever. The parting of the Red Sea was supposed to part them from all the ways of Egypt and the drowning of their enemies was to bring an end to their bitter slavery and lead to a glorious future. However, it was rather unfortunately the beginning of a very tumultuous relationship between God and Israel. The people of Israel did not understand that for the journey they were to undertake to the Promised Land in becoming a nation, they were going to need several different types of encounters.

Different encounters deform you by removing old habits allowing for reformation to take place bringing new ones (1 Cor 5:17). God wants us to have new wine in new wine skins or vessels. Depending on single or old encounters during a journey of many new turns means wrong application and unfortunate results. That is why even with experience, as good as it is in handling situations, it is relative and cannot be relied on above encounter because encounters alter experience.

The children of Israel failed so many times because they failed to grow in their relationship with God. One of the most unfortunate episodes borders around Moses leaving to meet with God (encounter) for a longer than expected period. The Israelites while waiting for longer than they imagined ended up committing idolatry because as I once heard, "they had left Egypt but Egypt hadn't left them". The miracles, signs and wonders that were performed in Egypt got their attention to follow God and be delivered from slavery however they lacked further encounters to transform them. As we are about to see this was caused by a much greater problem.

God has made an everlasting covenant with Abraham to prosper his descendants and make them a special people for His use and glory. Now after a long period of these people being enslaved, their cry was loud and reached to God and He remembered His covenant with Abraham. After Moses encountered God in the burning bush, he was given the assignment of delivering God's people from captivity in Egypt. It was during this battle for freedom that some of the greatest signs and wonders ever took place through Moses. Through this Moses achieved His assignment of removing God's people from bondage. After delivering the people out of slavery in Egypt Moses now had to take them to the Promised land. This is where He would experience some of His greatest struggles unfortunately ending with Himself being disqualified reaching the Promise. It is a tragedy that Moses found it easier liberating the Jews from Egypt than leading them to the Promise. I believe this is still true of us even today. We are able to give our lives to Christ after witnessing the mighty power of the Glorious God because we know we need saving. However, the problem becomes after our salvation, achieving and reaching God's plan and purpose for His life and enforcing the Promise of God in our lives. Like the Israelites, we live defeated lives even sometimes craving how life used to be, we change on the outside but are not able to be changed within for what the Promise of God demands.

Going back to the story of Exodus, the people saw God move, they saw and witnessed the great power of God working on their behalf. It is easy to understand their amazement of such a God, nothing similar had been seen before. They rightfully run to Him to be their God. However, the question is who they actually saw and followed, was it God or it was Moses? Yes, they saw such great acts but they were being performed by Moses. If only they had known Moses was just the vessel chosen, if only they had known he was just as human as them, if only they had known God was using Moses just to reach to them. God was not for Moses alone, but for them all. He was not God of Moses first, He was God of Israel. They never connected to Him that way because what they saw blocked what they should have known.

This same thing will keep happening in the life of Israel. Even after Moses died and Joshua continued, the story was largely the same. God usually seemed to be exclusive to and owned by an individual and the people at a distant obeying what seems to be the words of a man. This continued through the Judges to the kings and prophets. The one thing that stayed constant was the people of Israel failing God. In the history of Israel, there was a constant cycle that played out. There would be a God fearing leader who causes the people to repent and serve God or on the other hand an evil and wicked leader causing the people to turn from God. It was almost as if God was owned by the leader and the people did whatever the buyer at that time instructed and did. Why was this so with the people being under the mercy of the leader? Why was there no connection between the people themselves and their God? It was because of the problem of 'ownership of God'. The people themselves were slaves and beholden to their leaders because they refused to know God for themselves. Those who purposed to know God personally did not allow themselves to be led by the dictates of a wicked leader. When and where there is wrongful ownership of God, there is a large gap between people and God and individuals do not take time and effort to surrender their lives personally to God irrespective of the order of the day.

Unfortunately this same trend continued right through to the Pharisees and religious leaders of the New Testament where the ownership of God now became cemented in tradition. Temple worship gradually grew to a point where there were sects and various groups that dictated how worship of God must be. They prevented people from seeking God in heart, but it all became a set of actions with no meaning. It was worship God their way or no other way. Worship of God had been seized and the impossible had happened, individuals began to own God and control who and how we got to Him. The key to heaven seemingly was being controlled by men. Hard to imagine and difficult to swallow but a stark reality.

13

JESUS IS THE NEW LIFE

J esus came in with the NEW, that is the new covenant where there was no more changing of high priest. There will be no more office of the high priest and no more ownership of God. Jesus was sent to fix this problem of ownership once and for all. God was going to connect to all individually as He had originally wanted in the Garden of Eden. God of heaven and earth was going to use just one more person in the name of Jesus to finish His plan once and for all. Jesus came not to be just high priest as those who had come before but to introduce God to us in His most preferred name, Father. He Jesus is the only way to the Father.

Now forever and ever there will be no more reason to be disconnected or distant from God because Jesus is the Way forever. Jesus has also sent the Holy Spirit who is in every Christian and every believer to help us in all our needs in our relationship with Our Father. Now we must all go to God, not through Moses, Abraham, David nor anyone else. No, he does not belong to those people and isn't their God alone, He is our God, our Heavenly Father, who through Jesus has given us back direct access as it was in Eden. All people, tribes, languages, nations to call on the name of the Lord for salvation. Thanks be to God.

This does not mean God is no longer raising leaders. There is need of leaders who are to serve just as Jesus did. Jesus himself called and raised leaders at His time who became disciples and apostles used by God to lead and serve the church. However, Jesus is the last Saviour and true hero of all humanity, the one who God used to break every door and barrier previously manned by men. Now we are all just servants to lead people to the way, the only Way Jesus.

FINDING OUR PLACE IN LIFE

Life is like a movie script which keeps unfolding. The only one who knows the outcome of the movie is the director. Every other person involved in the movie must help by playing their various parts and roles however the direction and outcome of the movie is decided by the director. He makes all changes and decisions as seen fit to ensure the success of the movie in accordance with his vision.

God is the director of this life and He alone knows the entire script. The bible gives us certain insights into His script, important aspects that not only tell us about life itself but helps us to know more about the director too. A lot of people find it generally difficult relating to the bible. It represents different things to people; a history book, a book of laws and commands, a religious book and some even study it for intellectual reasons. How best is the bible to be used? The bible is best for knowing about God, which includes His plan for eternity and our place in it. From Genesis to Revelation the Word of God should be used to relate to God our Father and not for anything else.

This is important if we are to align to His script which has been already written. This is why the bible tells us He knows the end from the beginning and He is the Alpha and Omega. We cannot align to His eternal plan without knowing the director and what He expects of us.

If we are to be successful in our roles and contribute positively to God's plan, we cannot assume our own roles and responsibilities like a team without a coach or a company without a manager, but we must take time and effort to know the director and his wishes and expectations of us. No matter how much we think we can contribute out of our own will or capacity, we must allow ourselves to be led so our contributions are wholesome and long lasting. This is more important today in our fast-changing world where it can seem impossible to stay still or hold on. There's always something new happening, life is moving at such a fast pace and we must be careful so the right changes take place and not end up in a vicious cycle of temporary unnecessities. The right changes are the ones God instructs. If we lose our connection to the director, things can go wrong and fast, both in our personal lives and on a much broader scale. Simply put we need God. We must remember what Solomon said, calling everything vanity after going through every temporary pleasure on earth. It was never worth it, a life out of God's purpose no matter how pleasurable will have the wise still admit it doesn't add up to real satisfaction. He finally postured that the conclusion of all things is to fear God and follow Him.

WORSHIP, OUR WAY OF LIFE

Therefore, the most important thing a person can focus on is their worship of God. Whatever we worship is what controls us. Worship comes out of devotion and strong commitment. Our worship to God must be done in a personal and meaningful manner. It must be central to our lives making sure He is a part of everything we do and this will serve as a way of realigning wherever we find ourselves, even when we get into bad situations, like sheep with a shepherd we will find our way back. What becomes key is the way that we do this worship.

Worship is an age-old practice. It has and always will be a part of mankind. Over the course of history so many forms of worship have taken place and still does. Different mannerisms, different methods and different objects. In the olden days worship was mostly linked to deities and the cosmos for spiritual reasons but that has largely changed over time. Today, most people worship material things because of a lack of faith and it seems easier and more useful to concentrate on things that bring instant benefit. Worship of mountains and water bodies has been changed for money and technology. Instant gratification is the name of the game. We are often tempted to worship the creation over creator. Worship is eternal and anything that only has value in this life does not deserve to be worshipped.

Unfortunately, the tendency for humans is to worship even God in a material manner. We worship God for material reasons, that is for what we get or benefit. Our lack of understanding of God causes us to relate to Him wrongly. Our worship of Him must not be dependent on material things but must be moved by faith. Faith that He is a loving God who we entrust control of our lives to and as His children, our complete love for Him as our Father.

These days even we Christians can be tempted to worship God based on the beauty of a church building, its equipment, technology, elaborate programs and other reasons. Times are changing with new things constantly being introduced to enhance our worship experience but then we must pause and ask who is directing affairs and are those his wishes or ours.

We are told by Jesus that there is a time coming and has even now come where true worship will be properly defined. There was once a time where worship of God seemed exclusive to the Jewish people and at another time limited to a location. People of various backgrounds have always found a way of worshipping God that is influenced by their culture, both in style and form. The way we pray, the songs we sing and even the sermons we preach can be all influenced by where we come from. There are always changes taking place but when Jesus came he defined worship in its truest and final form.

Our Great and Mighty God who seeks to be personal wants to be worshipped in Spirit and truth. This is the purest form of worship. In Spirit, because it must not be dependent on anything material, in spirit so we can meet Him as He is in His sincerest form. In the beginning before the fall, worship was personal. God being Spirit visited man in the Garden for fellowship and what a beautiful experience that must have been. The very presence of God Himself one with His creation and children, what an atmosphere. After the fall worship took many forms that was not pleasing to God. God said to His prophet these people worship me with their mouth and not their heart. God had seen all forms of worship from sacrificing of animals, ritual and ceremonial worship, times and festivals and even idol worship. None of these were the best form of worship.

When you read the Psalms, there is something special about them. Its like getting a glimpse into the prayer and worship of many. We see how true, reverent, broken and real this worship is. Men and women of God longing for a deeper walk with God. All their heart being poured into the finding of this Great God. You picture that great worshipper David, in the secret place pouring out His heart and soul, glorifying His God with all He has.

But even with that, the greatest form of worship was still to come, a greater example. Jesus Christ the Son of God on the Cross, an image of sacrifice, complete devotion and commitment to the Father, both hands stretched out wide in surrender, chest bare before His God and Father, his heart yielded giving up everything He had including His spirit at the end of it all to His Father. This was the worship Jesus Himself had spoken about. This is total worship, God fully glorified.

Its not about the great worship concerts we have today, good as they are, oh how the greatest worship is found in secret places, teary eyed asking God for what you can do for Him. Allowing the writer of the script to give you His role even to the point of your life. Give Him your life, this is your reasonable worship as Paul stated.

14

IS CHRISTIANITY JUST ANOTHER RELIGION?

So the question becomes what is Christianity and is it just another religion?

We live in a world of many divisions such as nationality, colour, language etc. The same can be said when it comes to faith and spirituality, there are countless religions. It seems like there are several choices to pick from. God never expected Christianity to become one of them and even worse to enter competition with any of them. God always wanted more than religion. We are told of this in the New Testament where James explains what God sees as right religion.

> *26 If anyone among you thinks he is religious, and does not bridle his tongue but deceives his own heart, this one's religion is useless. 27 Pure and undefiled religion before God and the Father is this: to visit orphans and widows in their trouble, and to keep oneself unspotted from the world.*
> *James 1:27 NKJV*

Religion to God is not about an act or identifying with a larger group of people who share the same faith. God doesn't want religious people who take pride in just His name but don't live out their faith. We must realise what God wants and not just garner a religious lifestyle for the sake of it. Its not about carrying bibles, wearing Christian clothing or sticking scriptures on our vehicles. Its more than that. Lets see what God really desires.

He first established a nation in Israel that was to be set apart and consecrated unto Him and to be unlike any other nation. As written in 1 Peter 2:9 they were to be God's possession, a holy nation, chosen, a royal priesthood. Yes, and this is same for the church, we are to be a people for God and of God. But it gets even better than that. God didn't just choose Israel with the intention of forsaking the rest of the world. That isn't who God is. Israel was just His entry point to choose and start to separate a group of people onto Himself. Through Israel he planned to bring the Messiah who will save the world. He had a masterplan.

When God sent Jesus to redeem humanity, He wanted something more. He didn't just want a nation and people to Himself to serve and worship Him as we see in various kingdoms. He wanted something more unique. Jesus thereby came to establish a family for God, the children of God. A people that will be connected by a supernatural love sealed by the Spirit of God in us. This great plan of God had never been known in such detail until Jesus came and was leaving. In John 17 Jesus prayed for his disciples a very precious and real prayer revealing His heart for us. Before He declared that His people and followers will be known by the same love which He came to show on earth. He asked the Father for them to be One just as the Father was one with Him. The extraordinary love that made Jesus one with Father, the same unity was what He expected of His people, the church. A love that can be only from God. John 3:16 famously declares this kind of love. Jesus was setting up the basis on which this new kingdom will be built. Love and unity, ONENESS.

Christianity is not another religion. We are ONE family united by one Father and one Saviour who is the first born of this brethren. Jesus is the uniting factor in this family, the force that bonds all of us from different walks of life under our Father. This is how fellowship works, people bonded by the same shared faith in Jesus meeting to edify one another. We are supposed to be made better because of this family but this isn't always the case. This is due to our lack of understanding of family.

To understand what God is searching for, we must first look to understand the person of God. In the creation story, God is introduced as 'us', not singular but plural and that is because God is made up of the Father, the Son and the Holy Spirit. God the Father is introduced to Moses as 'YHWH' and 'I AM THAT I AM'. The Son is Jesus Christ the Messiah of the world. The Holy Spirit is the Helper, Comforter, the Spirit of Truth. All separate Persons but connecting perfectly together to be One. Three components that are so united they are impossible to divide and most often referred to as ONE name, GOD. Though they play separate roles and have different functions, they perfectly compliment and complete one another. They are each mindful of the hierarchy and do not interfere in each other's duty because they work in perfect synchrony like a perfect orchestra with no tune out of place. A whole book can be written explaining the perfection of the Godhead and still will not do it justice. The structural makeup of God can only be properly grasped by revelation given by the Spirit of God, it is a ONENESS unconceivable by the carnal mind and beyond our knowledge.

Now God created man in His image and similar likeness, and this carries great significance in understanding this family. God wants us to mirror Him and operate just like Him because that's how he made us. God functions as a family, as an inseparable unit and this is exactly how God purposed it for us. After God created the first man Adam, He observed and stated it is not good for man to be alone and sought to correct this by creating another being out of Adam. He brought out the woman from the man and this was the solution for the problem of loneliness.

During Creation, God realised there was a limitation on Adam even though He had been created in the image and likeness of God.

God Himself was a family, three persons all together making One, but Adam was just one person hence could not be a family or unit. He then took from Adam to create in his likeness as well. The reason God is not lonely is because He is structured as a family and operates as such, and Eve had to be added to Adam for this to complete our ability to be just like God. This is why man naturally gravitates towards the need for family.

All of creation, the birds, the fishes and land animals could not be suitable helpers because they were not in the same image and likeness as Adam. But Eve was taken out of the man and created by God. Just as God is in perfect unison, man could experience that same unity working together in purpose. This allows for completion and is God's original intention, what He desires for man. Out of His great love and heart He wanted nothing less for us than the completion He Himself experienced. When He commanded them to be fruitful and multiply it was to continue this family that He God had started. With Him being the example of perfect unison, this was to continue for eternity, the kingdom of God, the family of God. There was beautiful fellowship and everything was going to plan until the enemy of man showed up to circumvent the plan of God. This is why Satan hates family. This is why there are so many broken homes today. Just as Satan fought the family of God in the Garden, so is he still fighting the family of God today, and beyond our individual families which are units of the church, Satan will always seek ways of attacking the church of Jesus, the only legitimate family of God because of His Son Jesus.

Now after the fall Adam and Eve were removed from the garden and the Presence of God. The plan of God for man to operate just as Him was broken. With the knowledge of good and evil not only was it difficult for man to relate to God as He had intended but man could not even relate to his fellow man. This is unfortunately seen in the first family, in the children of Adam and Eve when Cain killed Abel. This was to be the beginning of many wicked, atrocious, heinous and abominable acts man would do towards fellow man.

Humanity has truly gone through several painful periods where God just like in the time of Noah has been heartbroken at what has gone on in His creation. Wars will continue in all levels of society until there is a restoration and return to God's original agenda for man, Family.

15

THE FAMILY OF GOD

Jesus did not come to establish another religion because it is not the answer. When Jesus declared it is finished on the cross it meant He was the final answer, nothing else. There would be no other way so this was to be the only way once and for all!

Jesus refused to be made a king because He did not seek an earthly kingdom nor subjects. He was not even interested in being high priest or one of the religious leaders. He referred to His disciples as His brothers even though they revered Him and knew Him as Rabbi and more. Everything Jesus did on earth was towards the furtherance and building of the kingdom of God. He knew and understood that what He belonged to was the only and one true kingdom. He had no interest in anything that wasn't eternal.

After His crucifixion and resurrection before He ascended to Heaven and back to the Father, He gave one last command. Just as God had instructed Adam and Eve to be fruitful and multiply, Jesus told His disciples to go out to the ends of the earth making disciples of all men. Jesus had spent His years in ministry establishing disciples and starting a new family out of Himself, being the second Adam. He was the new man sent from God for the salvation of man and He started with the twelve and then also sent them out while He was with them, being trained to also make disciples. As the day of his Ascension to heaven drew nearer, Jesus was focused on passing over the mantle of discipleship to those who followed Him. They were to not only be disciples of Christ but apostles of the gospel message. He had made disciples of them, pouring Himself into them so they could be of His image and likeness. Jesus directed His disciples to wait for the Helper, The Holy Spirit of God who came on the day of Pentecost. This was the last piece of the puzzle, the breath of God coming as a wind to all the disciples sealing their confirmation as sons and daughters of the most High God, the seal of the family of God. With the image and likeness of Jesus and the breath of God through the Holy Spirit indwelling in them, this would be the child of God, a member of His family and partaker of His everlasting kingdom. The mission and purpose to be fruitful and multiply making disciples out of all men. The invitation now not by birth into a nation but by rebirth through Jesus, reborn of the Spirit of God. Anyone and everyone invited to join this great family of God. The original mandate of God for man reinstituted. This is the same purpose for you and I today who have been saved by the blood of Jesus into His family. Not religion, no cults, not even denominations or the many dividing lines but the real family of God only seen by the mark of Christ through discipleship and the living breath of God, a Spirit filled life. Hallelujah.

What we must understand is everyone is looking for family, somewhere to belong because of the original makeup of man as earlier seen. This is the purpose of God, the purpose of creation. God had a plan for all creation, and man as well to have and feel a sense of belonging. Just as all animals know where they belong, even more so with us. This need to belong to a family is why Jesus came to the world, looking for those who need one to give them the best choice ever with the best Father. It is not a family like the ones we see on earth, broken down, scattered and full of so many problems because of the presence of evil in them. God knows the need of true family where He is Head, the Good Father. Every being needs family that nurtures the heart and soul and this is what Jesus came to establish. Not one designed along tribal lines, politics, occupation, education etc. or any of all these other things that break humans along lines and levels. The only thing important in this family is our longing for the Kingdom of God and its success. Not selfish ambitions but Godly purpose, that's why its God's family and not ours. Not a building or place that we can go in and out, activating it like a membership card. Not a Sunday churchgoer who just marks attendance, This is a Family for everyday. A family beyond the church building, a family who dines with one another. Just look at the early church, doing everything with each other in mind. The golden rule of loving the other. Selling their goods and possessions for the collective good. We cannot comprehend that today because there's no such family, so much divisions but you and I would still gladly do it for those we think we love and are deserving of it.

The problem is sadly and unfortunately the church of God seems to have come even worse than the families of the world. The way we attend church today makes us seem like strangers, it does not build trust and allows for hypocrisy. We don't take time to properly know each other and build the kind of family God will be proud of. How we ought to each be true and honest with ourselves and ask whether we are for the kingdom's cause or for our individual gains. Like Ananias and Sapphira, we cannot fool the Holy Spirit, who is the seal of the family and judgement will be sure to come and it won't be pretty. Let's review our motives and intents for wanting to be God's Children and part of His beloved family and make sure our heart remains for God and His church. Our heart must beat for His Church, our family. Amen.

16

THE SIGNIFICANCE OF THE CROSS OF JESUS

To every believer this is the turning point from shallow to deep waters, being firmly rooted. The understanding of what the cross means is what leaves an indelible mark on the Christian. Just you before the cross, nothing else, no distractions, just you. What does it mean to you? This is what is known as conviction. This is what enables a Christian to be a suitable and helpful contributor to the family of God. Otherwise it is possible to just be a part of the family, having a negative rather than positive impact. It is like a family member who neglects the family he belongs to, causing it to be broken and rather blessing someone else's. The impact the Cross of Jesus must have on each believer is key to properly belong to the family of God.

The power of the cross is unmatched in bringing an individual's heart into submission to the One who bore the cross, Jesus Christ. There are many different reasons for one coming into knowledge of the saving grace of the Lord Jesus such as life's difficulties, being invited to a church program or being evangelised to by a family member. However, before one can be imprinted permanently with the mark of Christ, the true meaning of the cross must be established. This is the power of God that knocks at the hardness of our heart breaking every bit of resistance, transforming and preparing it by the love of Christ for God to enter in. This process is like a spiritual heart transplant necessary for the new you to be released.

You see you can become a Christian by confessing and giving yourself to Christ, inviting Him as your Lord and Saviour while still maintaining and having the same hardness of the old heart. This ultimately leads to refusing to receive God wholly and in all His ways. There will always be some resistance and opposition to God, it will always seem like a fight to serve God and this causes spiritual fatigue wearing you out. This often results in defeated Christianity living and ultimately compromise. God does not like this and declares his opposition to people being lukewarm, He wants people to either be hot or cold.

> *So then, because you are lukewarm, and neither cold nor hot, I will vomit you out of My mouth. Rev 3:16 NKJV*

WALKING IN VICTORY THROUGH CHRIST

God already has a procedure to help His children walk in victory. It is not up to us to suffer through this life trying to be like our Father and to identify as His. He as the Good Father has already made a way.

> *Then will I sprinkle clean water upon you, and ye shall be clean: from all your filthiness, and from all your idols, will I cleanse you.*

> *A new heart also will I give you, and a new spirit will I put within you: and I will take away the stony heart out of your flesh, and I will give you an heart of flesh.*

58

And I will put my spirit within you, and cause you to walk in my statutes, and ye shall keep my judgments, and do them.

Ezekiel 36:25-27 NLT

This scripture reveals God's major role in our redemption. God can be seen to be very active, the one taking charge of the process. It can be broken down into three parts. In the first part God washes us, cleansing us of all filth and dirt, seeking to remove whatever it is messing our identity. He doesn't mistake the dirt for who we are, knowing we are able to be made clean and not whatever circumstances we come in. These are all the things that came because of our past. This is to deal with shame, guilt and anything that prevents us from the hope of a glorious future.

Luke 15:20 And he arose, and came to his father. But when he was yet a great way off, his father saw him, and had compassion, and ran, and fell on his neck, and kissed him.

Luke 15:21 And the son said unto him, Father, I have sinned against heaven, and in thy sight, and am no more worthy to be called thy son.

Luke 15:22 But the father said to his servants, Bring forth the best robe, and put it on him; and put a ring on his hand, and shoes on his feet (NLT)

Like the story of the prodigal son God is eagerly awaiting the return of all His children. He does not plan to leave us the way we came but clean us up restoring us to the original beauty and splendor. The Father knew His son wasn't what he had gone and become but knew who he truly was so rejoiced at his return. Rather than punishment, he washes us and changes our garment so we do not feel ashamed and can identify with our Father.

> *Luke 15:24 For this my son was dead, and is alive again; he was lost, and is found. And they began to be merry.*

Notice the reason for the rejoicing. The son just like us was dead and lost during all those years of living life according to our own ways and pleasures, serving all forms of idols in the process. Returning back home to our Father turns as back to the narrow path of eternal life and is worth rejoicing. We unfortunately may get lost often times in this life of so many paths but that is not who we are or supposed to be, the real us is found when we return back home. He is waiting to wash us.

Secondly God works on our heart, knowing well any external change must be reflected on the inside. As seen from Isaiah 36:26 above, it's imperative that every child of God has a change of heart, exchanging our hardened and stony heart for new ones that are fashioned after His. The old heart has all the old ways in which we went after the wrong things. The new heart is for the new you. This will then allow and enable us to follow His ways that are right and glorious.

Failure to go through this process creates an imbalance and the Christian staggers throughout their walk on earth and will fail to look like they belong to the family of God.

17

HOW GOD GIVES US A NEW HEART

Coming before the Cross of Jesus Christ gets us on our knees. We are confronted with the picture of undeserved sacrifice for us and this brings us to the gate of repentance. Our hearts confronted with the knowledge that the Saviour of the world, the Son of God gave His very life for the salvation of ours.

It is so unfathomable how much value God places on us to do this. Jesus going through so much pain and suffering from the very people He came to save, even being rejected by His own people and actually crucified by them. Yet God so wanted us in His family, and not as subjects or servants but as first class citizens. We are not just anybody like we see citizens being in some countries, we are of the greatest value to them.

The importance of properly going through this step of the Cross is for brokenness. The Cross breaks us entirely starting with our heart which is where the Spirit of the Lord loves to dwell.

Psalms 51:17 The sacrifices of God are a broken spirit: a broken and a contrite heart, O God, thou wilt not despise. NLT

The Cross is where our conviction begins. The heart acts as a kind of door to the body. As discussed earlier the heart spreads whatever is in it throughout the body. So, a haughty heart acts as a blockade to your body not easily allowing anything new inside but a broken heart allows for the Spirit to take over. The Holy Spirit, the Spirit of truth is able to enter a broken heart and take over and use the vessel magnificently. Pride is abominable to the Spirit of God. There are numerous scriptures showing God's opposition to pride.

> *James 4:6 But he giveth more grace. Wherefore he saith, God resisteth the proud, but giveth grace unto the humble. NLT*

> *Psalms 138:6 Though the LORD be high, yet hath he respect unto the lowly: but the proud he knoweth afar off. NLT*

God has a soft spot for the lowly and broken. Those that fail to pass through the Cross leaves pride intact. The Cross is the end of flesh and opens us to the Spirit of God. The Cross is the place of repentance. The Cross is where the heart is changed. The Cross is where we truly walk into a new life in Christ, broken before Him but ready to be used to His glory.

> *And I will put my spirit within you, and cause you to walk in my statutes, and ye shall keep my judgments, and do them. Isaiah 36:27 NLT*

The third part of the scripture in Isaiah is God giving us His Spirit to help us to be like Him and to know His ways. If we have His Spirit, we become like Him, know what He knows and will do the things He does.

Below is Jesus telling us about the work of this Spirit:

"But in fact, it is best for you that I go away, because if I don't, the Advocate won't come. If I do go away, then I will send him to you. And when he comes, he will convict the world of its sin, and of God's righteousness, and of the coming judgment. The world's sin is that it refuses to believe in me. Righteousness is available because I go to the Father, and you will see me no more. Judgment will come because the ruler of this world has already been judged. "There is so much more I want to tell you, but you can't bear it now. When the Spirit of truth comes, he will guide you into all truth. He will not speak on his own but will tell you what he has heard. He will tell you about the future. He will bring me glory by telling you whatever he receives from me."

John 16:7-14 NLT

The Spirit of God, the Holy Spirit does the convicting work. He becomes the central part of our lives in a very real way. Once you walk well with Him which is truth, you will never feel alone or have to walk the journey by yourself. He becomes your enabler. He is Jesus with you.

Have you ever tried to use your mind to worship God? It quickly becomes very stale no matter how it might have seemed in the beginning. The reason is in a very key scripture in Jesus' sermon on the mount of Olives.

The pure in heart will see God. Matthew 5:8 NLT

This is not speaking of when we die and see Him in heaven but about our Christian walk. God has given us the chance to see Him now while on earth.

*"If you had really known me, you would know who my
Father is. From now on, you do know him and have
seen him!" Philip said, "Lord, show us the Father,
and we will be satisfied." Jesus replied, "Have I been
with you all this time, Philip, and yet you still don't
know who I am? Anyone who has seen me has seen the
Father! So why are you asking me to show him to you?"*

John 14:7-9 NLT

Jesus told His disciples who asked to see God the Father that
once they had seen Him Jesus they had seen the Father. This is the
same for us today. Through the purification of our heart scripture
tells us we would see God. As our hearts become pure through the
finished work of the Cross, the eyes of our hearts are opened and we
gradually see and realize the object of our worship. This personalizes
our worship making it become real, an experience. Tangible. The
mind is switched off during such an experience and all staleness
leaves. This however only starts from the heart, and not just any
heart but the pure one.

Now none of us have naturally pure hearts after the fall but our
hearts are described as desperately wicked (Jeremiah 17:9), definitely
hearts that cannot see God. Anyone who decides to worship God
Almighty with this type of heart only does so in the flesh but even
worse, if they persist feels so distant and disconnected from the
object of worship because you can't see Him. Worship cannot be
spiritually blind but must be awakening. There's a light that removes
all darkness.

*"The Lord's light penetrates the human spirit, exposing
every hidden motive." Proverbs 20:27 NLT*

This light, the same light from the beginning when God said
let there be light. The illumination of man. When this light comes,

conviction follows for where light dwells, darkness cannot. Light convicts or arrests the darkness and this will continue until light spreads all over. This light comes from the fire in our hearts, lit by the Holy Spirit. That is why God wants us hot, not lukewarm, or cold. That is a life of conviction, a life on fire for God.

> *"I know all the things you do, that you are neither hot nor cold. I wish that you were one or the other! But since you are like lukewarm water, neither hot nor cold, I will spit you out of my mouth!"*

> *Revelation 3:15-16 NLT*

Let's just take one story from the Bible, one of my favourite prophets and one of my favourite scriptures.

> *"But if I say I'll never mention the Lord or speak in his name, his word burns in my heart like a fire. It's like a fire in my bones! I am worn out trying to hold it in! I can't do it!"*

> *Jeremiah 20:9 NLT*

Prophet Jeremiah regardless of how much persecution He was under, no matter how much he tried to be quiet about God, realized he was not able to. The fire, the conviction, the force inside Him couldn't allow him keep quiet. No matter how much pressure the enemy put, no matter the force of his own flesh, nothing was able to resist the power of that fire. Conviction wouldn't allow him be lukewarm or indifferent.

The Christian cannot look to the cross and live defeated and powerless and even worse indifferent lives. The cross of Jesus convicts, recharges and keeps the believer going. Whether through storms or gales, the Christian has such power to overcome, because what is impossible for men is not impossible to God. It's not just wearing crosses as fashion or hanging them all around but the cross breaks a normal human being transforming Him to a supernatural powerhouse for God Almighty by the power of the Holy Spirit. May the cross continually break us till we have no more of us but only Him.

18

CREATING THE RIGHT ATMOSPHERE AROUND YOU

There is something known in science as atmospheric pressure. It is basically the amount of pressure the air around us exerts on a surface. Now the higher a person climbs, say while mountain climbing the lower the pressure while at sea level the pressure is higher. This air pressure is naturally around all of us and becomes a part of our atmosphere however it varies depending on factors such as location and altitude. We can learn something from this when it comes to creating a divine atmosphere around you. Just like with atmospheric pressure, with a child of God, there are also unseen elements that surround you to create a divine atmosphere. A divine atmosphere is one of supernatural advantage where spiritually you are surrounded with the right climate for victorious Christian living. Before Jesus left to be crucified, He knew He would be physically leaving them but wanted to leave them something supernatural that will be of great benefit to them for the work they were to do. The world can be a brutal place to live with troubles everywhere, the world is even more unfriendly to the Christian. Whether it is a difficult marriage, workplace stress or even spiritual attacks life can sometimes get the better of us. It is at that point you need peace the most, a supernatural peace that seems to relatively fade every storm away. Just as Jesus was sleeping in the storm while the disciples were afraid and crying for their lives, there's a place where a person is perfectly sound despite all life may throw at them. This is peace beyond understanding and this was what Jesus left with His disciples. (John 14:27) We are assured that we have the same peace that enabled Jesus to live victoriously on earth, pleasing the Father and carrying out His God given assignment.

Nothing pleases the enemy more than to steal the joy and peace from our lives leaving us oppressed, dejected and ultimately depressed. He looks for whatever possible way to add stress into our lives, so we always feel like we are fighting for our sanity. No one wants to be fighting forever. This is why we must create a divine atmosphere around us with the Holy Spirit at the gate determining what enters. We are reminded of Paul who went through countless suffering yet declared that God's grace was sufficient. He yet again declared He can do all things through Christ who strengthens Him. He was walking in a supernatural realm where he rose above all earthly things. This enabled Him finish well.

I have fought the good fight, I have finished the race,
I have kept the faith. 2 Timothy 4:7 NKJV

Scripture directs us to pray without ceasing. This is to pray continually staying in constant communication with the Father. It is very dangerous to get out of touch and reach of the Father. This is why it's important to have the necessary atmosphere around you that allows for this constant fellowship. This the enemy will do all he can to prevent. If he can get you out of the garden into the wilderness, he believes he has the advantage. Anytime you must even go to the wilderness, you must take the atmosphere of God with you.

Each individual must develop a way to allow for the sweet presence of God to stay around you especially for the wellbeing of your heart. For a heart to be at peace, one must be at rest despite the natural circumstances. It is not pretending or ignoring of truth, but living by a higher faith according to the promise of God. Staying in this atmosphere ensures we enjoy all of the benefits God gives his children such as favour, strength, healing, hope, and belief. There are many advantages a Christian receives through this presence, too many to name. I have heard so many testimonies of normal people achieving great unthinkable feats by staying in the presence of God.

Prayer is key in establishing this. Not moments of prayer, but ceaseless always. Prayer can be audible or in your heart, once you are praying that's what matters. Praying in the spirit is always a very useful tool especially when your divine atmosphere seems under attack. That is when you have your spiritual language which is praying in other tongues is very useful. When our minds are so active, zoning out to pray can be very tough and that is when praying by faith and allowing the Spirit lead you to pray in other tongues is so valuable (Rom 8:26-28). Paul declared how edifying it can be (1 Cor 14:4).

Our enemy the adversary will always seek to destroy this presence around us so we begin to walk as just anyone. He knows very well our advantage over him is held in keeping this presence and carrying this divine atmosphere. I like to picture it like a bubble of grace where we are surrounded by all the beautiful blessings once we stay in. Whether it's keeping spirit filled music with you, listening to the anointed word of God or praying to revitalise yourself in the night hours, do whatever it personally takes to walk in this divine presence. You must be able to create your own activities out of church hours to ensure you don't dwindle out of God's presence. Jesus made it clear that His peace He gives is different from the one the world gives (John 14:27). Remember to not quench the spirit, the beautiful presence of God. (1 Thessalonians 5:16-19). Do not stray into the world as a believer. Stay different.

19

DON'T STAY IN THE BOAT

t must be absolutely stated that the enemy is not afraid of this kind of wholesale Christianity no matter how high the numbers. The Bible says they who know their God shall do exploits. It is the strength of each believer and not just the strength in numbers. Even in heaven it is amazing to think that Satan was able to get a third of the angels to fall with him.

> *And there was war in heaven: Michael and his angels fought against the dragon; and the dragon fought and his angels,*
>
> *And prevailed not; neither was their place found any more in heaven.*
>
> *And the great dragon was cast out, that old serpent, called the Devil, and Satan, which deceiveth the whole world: he was cast out into the earth, and his angels were cast out with him.*
>
> *Revelations 12:7-9*

So even in heaven it wasn't about the number of angels but the quality of understanding each had about why they were there. How connected were they to God that when war broke out between the angels, many found themselves on the wrong side against God. The thing is each had to know it for themselves, it had to be personal and not just another angel out of the myriad of them. If this once took place in heaven then why do we think it any different on earth? When judgement day arrives, we are told it's not who you say you are nor what you say you did. Your work will pass through fire to test the quality because that's what it's about.

The one thing stronger than the enemy is conviction. In the story of Job, he was confronted with an enemy he didn't know nor could understand. Satan had challenged God concerning the integrity of Job's worship after God had pointed it out. As a result of this Job was put through immeasurable pain and suffering by the enemy. But after the enemy had destroyed all Job had including his health, Job still declared his hope in God.

> *Though he slay me, yet will I trust in him: but I will maintain mine own ways before him.*
>
> *He also shall be my salvation: for an hypocrite shall not come before him.*
>
> *Job 13:15-16*

The New Living Translation puts it this way:

> *"God might kill me, but I have no other hope. I am going to argue my case with him. But this is what will save me—I am not godless. If I were, I could not stand before him."*
>
> *Job 13:15-16 NLT*

No matter what was to happen, even in the midst of confusion about all that had happened, Job will trust and hope ONLY in God. He would take His case to ONLY God because there was no other option. Like the widow who persisted and persevered at the door of the wicked judge till she got a favourable answer, Job understood God was His only hope and the only One He could trust. So he had no one else to plead his case to but God Almighty no matter what happened. Job had shown God was not just an option but His only choice. Like the three Hebrew boys who told King Nebuchadnezzar that they would worship no other god no matter what because God is able to save them but even if He doesn't, they will still worship only the true God (Daniel 3). This is conviction, when you remove every other option and just have one.

We are told the kingdom of God is like a man who saw treasure and sold everything he had to buy the field. This is the type of conviction God seeks which comes from the value on what you believe. This is faith at work which no enemy can stand. The greatest type of conviction comes from deep faith born out of relationship with God. One that continuously develops, one that has passed through the highs and lows. A relationship does not only consist of the good but the bad too. Peter speaks about this when speaking of endurance and what it builds.

> *"So be truly glad. There is wonderful joy ahead, even though you must endure many trials for a little while. These trials will show that your faith is genuine. It is being tested as fire tests and purifies gold—though your faith is far more precious than mere gold. So when your faith remains strong through many trials, it will bring you much praise and glory and honor on the day when Jesus Christ is revealed to the whole world."*

1 Peter 1:6-7 NLT

King David exemplifies this type of relationship with the strong connection he had with God. The Message Bible describes Him as one whose heart beats after God's heart (Acts 13:22). God knew David was always searching for His heart and this pleased Him. No wonder David was the one who purposed to build God a house. He truly cared for His God and looked for ways to show his love and please Him.

To understand the type of relationship we must desire, let's study common human behaviour. The relationship between mother and baby comes very naturally and the reliance the baby has on the mother is not taught. However, with each year that passes there's a realization that this once natural connection must now be developed and grown if the relationship is to be sustained. Failure to do so risks the relationship breaking or being negatively affected. Growth must go along with maturity. Paul once declared when I was a child I thought like a child but now I'm an adult I've put childish things behind (1 Corinthians 13:11). The way a baby relates to a mother differs from when that same baby becomes a teenager and again an adult. It is inappropriate for an adult or teenager to breastfeed. Just because it was once acceptable does not mean it will always be. This is how maturity works.

In the same way our relationship with God must develop if we are to succeed in our walk with Him. We cannot afford to limit ourselves by constantly comparing to how we started.

Ecclesiastes 7:10 Say not thou, What is the cause that the former days were better than these? for thou dost not enquire wisely concerning this. KJV

Things will not always remain the same. Don't get stuck in yesterday but push on for a better and new. Remember God is a God of new things. We cannot always pray, fast or worship the same way we started. Don't let time, style or other such qualities become a basis for stagnation. But increasingly allow the Spirit of God to have His way in stretching you to go deeper and closer to God. It may not be comfortable but it is to our advantage for it will increase the quality of our relationship with our Father. This is what becomes our testimony and our victory.

> *Revelation 12:11 And they overcame him by the blood of the Lamb, and by the word of their testimony; and they loved not their lives unto the death.*

Our testimony is our continuous growth and betterment in our walk with Him. Every season brings a new testimony. Once we were strangers and enemies to Him but now we are part of His family.

Our walk with God must not become stagnant. At whatever level of relationship we are, we must endeavour to push deeper. A favourite worship song of mine speaks about the closer one gets to God, the more we see and the more we desire. Actually, this is echoed in several worship hymns and songs which come from the Psalms. Taste and see that the Lord is Good (Psalm 34:8).

So wherever you find yourself today in your relationship with Him, whether yet to begin a relationship with God, at the early stages, maturing, backslidden or angry at the world, God and you know for yourself where you really are. It is not the end. Wherever you find yourself know that God is desirous of a real and serious relationship, one that is centred on truth. Not with anyone else but just you. I am reminded of the story of Peter. He believed he loved the Lord and longed for ways to show it. When he saw Jesus walking on water, he desired same, that same level wanting to be able to do what His Lord could. That's what fellowship is and what it does. You want to imitate what you see. Jesus invited him out to join Him and do likewise, to walk on water. But when Peter removed his gaze from Jesus and saw the storm he began to drown. Jesus questioned why he doubted and didn't believe. His faith fell short.

The storms of life will come hard and the enemy will roar like a lion to get our attention and keep it from God. We will like Peter waver in our faith and have unbelief, but let that not stop us from always getting out of the boat of stagnation to fellowship with Jesus. Let us not be comfortable in the boat but yearn for all Jesus has for us. He's always inviting us to the deep, the miraculous. He will always catch us for those who fall and we must continue to desire the deep end no matter how few are able to reach. Don't settle for the shore for a deeper walk Is what will develop us making us to be more like Him, doing the things He did and being who He was.

May we all do all we can so we may echo the same words as Paul

"I have fought a good fight, I have finished my course, I have kept the faith:"

2 Timothy 4:7 KJV

A heart like yours is my desire. Amen.

20

THE PROMISE WE HOLD TO

You got to be confident in your relationship with God. You got to know for yourself you have a relationship with God the Father, God the Son and God the Holy Spirit. Romans 8:16 tells us the Spirit testifies with our own spirit that we are children of God. You must know you belong to God just as Jesus knew He was the Son of God to walk in His victory. This becomes the inner witness you need to help you walk this life. It gets lonely at times and in those times when it feels no one is there for you or they just not enough, you need something greater and more to help you through those moments. That is when you must rely on your relationship with God. Hebrews 4:16 directs us to come boldly before God's throne of grace to find mercy and help when we need it. It is a boldness that God is with you. One must be bold to know God, to get closer, to feel Him, to forget yourself and come into His presence. Just like coming before a great king, seeking the audience of the King of Kings can be overwhelming but it's rewarding. He is a rewarder of those that diligently seek Him. It is necessary that you must know this for yourself in every fibre of your being.

We all go through difficult moments in our Christian journeys where the temptation to lose faith and doubt God waxes strong but we must not give in. With the right investment in your relationship with God, your spirit will never let you go because God holds on to your spirit. No matter how much your flesh may doubt and your soul may question, your spirit is tied to the Spirit of God. Your heart feels nowhere better than in the love of God. You seek and yearn for His presence and fellowship and it becomes an integral part of your life. God is personal is no figment of the imagination. He needs to be more than real in your life driving your actions, your purpose and vision. When He becomes the centre of your life, you revolve in the right direction.

God has done everything in His power to give us abundant life. He has loved us with an everlasting love and wants to be with us for eternity. This earth is fleeting and will pass away. We are just passing through and on the way to permanent life with Him. We only see and know in part but when all this is done, we will see the full picture. We will see God in His true Glory, oh happy day. Jesus is preparing our mansions and houses, oh the joy of that day when all things will be made new. In conclusion please lets read the following scripture:

Now I saw a new heaven and a new earth, for the first heaven and the first earth had passed away. Also there was no more sea. Then I, John, saw the holy city, New Jerusalem, coming down out of heaven from God, prepared as a bride adorned for her husband. And I heard a loud voice from heaven saying, "Behold, the tabernacle of God is with men, and He will dwell with them, and they shall be His people. God Himself will be with them and be their God. And God will wipe away every tear from their eyes; there shall be no more death, nor sorrow, nor crying. There shall be no more pain, for the former things have passed away."

Then He who sat on the throne said, "Behold, I make all things new." And He said to me, "Write, for these words are true and faithful." Rev 21:1-5 NKJV

I want to announce to every reader that God has an amazing plan for us. He is coming back for us but we have not been left alone till then. He is still in charge of His creation and through us He seeks to carry out His good plans and save as many souls from eternal damnation. We have a promise of eternal life we must hold on to at all cost exchanging it for nothing. Through our relationship with Him, He will ensure we make it. He wants us more than we want Him. Relationship with Him will show you that. God bless you as you start to make a new decision for Him.

ABOUT THE AUTHOR

Edem is a man with a heart for God. He's a deep thinker and this cuts across everything he does. Having served in different capacities at church, he found a strong passion as a youth pastor helping young people find themselves through a relationship with God. He is currently an assistant at Salvation Bible Outreach in the Eastern Region of Ghana. He is an engineer by profession and works as a production manager at Shecco Tiles, a family owned brick manufacturing company. His strong love for God comes through all he does. Calm and quiet, he enjoys nature especially the beach spending time around people he loves. He is usually caught meditating and writing in his spare time.